P9-CSA-188

Avon Public Library
280 West Main Street
Avon, MA 02322

★ It's My State! ★ ★ ★ ★ ★

IOWA

The Hawkeye State

David C. King and Jackie F. Stanmyre

Cavendish Square

New York

Published in 2017 by Cavendish Square Publishing, LLC
243 5th Avenue, Suite 136, New York, NY 10016

Copyright © 2017 by Cavendish Square Publishing, LLC

Third Edition

No part of this publication may be reproduced, stored in a retrieval system, or transmitted in any form or by any means—electronic, mechanical, photocopying, recording, or otherwise—without the prior permission of the copyright owner. Request for permission should be addressed to Permissions, Cavendish Square Publishing, 243 5th Avenue, Suite 136, New York, NY 10016. Tel (877) 980-4450; fax (877) 980-4454.

Website: cavendishsq.com

This publication represents the opinions and views of the author based on his or her personal experience, knowledge, and research. The information in this book serves as a general guide only. The author and publisher have used their best efforts in preparing this book and disclaim liability rising directly or indirectly from the use and application of this book.

CPSIA Compliance Information: Batch #CS16CSQ

All websites were available and accurate when this book was sent to press.

Library of Congress Cataloging-in-Publication Data

Names: King, David C., author. | Stanmyre, Jackie F., author.
Title: Iowa / David C. King and Jackie F. Stanmyre.
Description: New York : Cavendish Square Publishing, 2016. | Series: It's my state! | Includes index. | Description based on print version record and CIP data provided by publisher; resource not viewed.
Identifiers: LCCN 2015050830 (print) | LCCN 2015048867 (ebook) | ISBN 9781627132404 (ebook) | ISBN 9781627132381 (library bound)
Subjects: LCSH: Iowa--Juvenile literature.
Classification: LCC F621.3 (print) | LCC F621.3 .K564 2016 (ebook) | DDC 977.7--dc23
LC record available at http://lccn.loc.gov/2015050830

Editorial Director: David McNamara
Editor: Fletcher Doyle
Copy Editor: Nathan Heidelberger
Art Director: Jeffrey Talbot
Designer: Joseph Macri
Senior Production Manager: Jennifer Ryder-Talbot
Photo Research: J8 Media

The photographs in this book are used by permission and through the courtesy of: RogersPhotography/Shutterstock.com, cover; Kenneth M. Highfill, 4; Steve Maslowski, 4; Max Sudakov/Shutterstock.com, 4; Joseph SohmVisions of America/Photodisc/Getty Images, 5; Evilwop66/File:Granite Marker.jpg/Wikimedia Commons, 5; Mark A. Schneider, 5; Igor Kovalenko/Shutterstock.com, 6; Alex Maclean/Getty Images, 8; Julie Habel, 9; Joseph Sohm/ChromoSohm Inc., 9; Accurate Art, 10; Tom Bean, 13; Danita Delimont/Gallo Images/Getty Images, 14; AP Photo/The Telegraph Herald, Dave Kettering, 14; Ben Franske/File:Grotto of the Redemption.jpg/Wikimedia Commons, 14; Marshall Astor modified by Xiaphias/File:Iowa80interior.png Wikimedia Commons, 15; AP Photo/The Gazette, Laura Segall, 15; GardenLover2008/File:RG Lake Helen.jpg/Wikimedia Commons, 15; The Image Works: Andre Jenny, 16; Gregory K. Scott, 17; axnjax/iStockphoto.com, 18; Ty Smedes Nature, 19; Rod Planck, 20; Michael P. Gadomski, 20; Art Wolfe/Getty Images, 20; DEA / G. Cappelli/DeAgostini/Getty Images, 21; Critterbiz/Shutterstock.com, 21; Wildnerdpix/Shutterstock.com, 21; SD Dirk/Mississippi River viewed from Julien Dubuque Monument site 3180/Flickr.com, 22; Ty Smedes Nature, 24; North Wind Picture Archives, 25; MPI/Getty Images, 26; North Wind Picture Archives, 28; Tim Thompson, 29; North Wind Picture Archives, 32; MPI/Getty Images, 33; Tom Bean, 34; AP Photo/Waterloo Courier, Rick Chase, 34; Wolterk/iStock Editorial/Thinkstock, 35; Walter Bibikow, 35; Joseph Sohm/ChromoSohm Inc., 36; Hulton Archive/Getty Images, 37; Chicago History Museum/Getty Images, 38; Bettmann, 39; Lake County Museum, 40; Jake Hukee/Shutterstock.com, 41; Kirk Edwards/Taxi/Getty Images, 44; Hulton-Deutsch Collection, 46; age fotostock, 47; Interim Archives/Getty Images, 48; Harry How/Getty Images for USOC, 48; AFP/Getty Images, 48; Chris Polk, 49; Bettmann, 49; Jason Merritt/Getty Images Entertainment/Thinkstock, 49; Accurate Art, 50; Matthew Holst/Getty Images, 52; Rue des Archives /Collection PVDE/Getty Images, 53; Tom Bean, 54; AP Photo/Waterloo Courier, Rick Chase, 54; Lindsay Hebberd, 54; MCT via Getty Images, 55; Ty Smedes Nature, 55; Thinkstock/Stockbyte/Getty Images, 56; Madeleine Openshaw/Shutterstock.com, 59; Daniel Acker/Bloomberg via Getty Images, 60; Rich Koele/Shutterstock.com, 62; Chris Polk, 62; MPI/Getty Images, 62; © Lyroky/Alamy Stock Photo, 64; © Grant Heilman Photography/Alamy Stock Photo, 66; Annie Griffiths Belt/CORBIS, 67; Spencer Platt/Getty Images, 68; Walter Bibikow, 68; Scott Camazine, 89; Corbis, 69; tacar/Shutterstock.com, 70; Envision: Mark Ferri, 71; Tom Bean, 73; Ian Worpole, 74; Denis Jr. Tangney/E+/Getty Images, 75; © Lyroky/Alamy Stock Photo, 75.

Printed in the United States of America

IOWA
CONTENTS

A QUICK LOOK AT

State Flower: Wild Rose

The wild rose was selected as the state flower in 1897, though no specific type of wild rose was singled out. However, many Iowans think of the wild prairie rose as the state flower. Prairie roses bloom from June to late summer in different shades of pink. Pioneers heading west often decorated their wagons with the colorful blossoms.

State Bird: Eastern Goldfinch

The eastern goldfinch is sometimes called the American goldfinch. These birds make their homes throughout the state. A male eastern goldfinch has bright yellow feathers on most of its body and black feathers on its head and wings. Female goldfinches are usually yellow and brown. The eastern goldfinch was made the state bird in 1933.

State Tree: Oak

The Iowa state legislature chose the oak as the state tree in 1961. Different types of oak trees thrive throughout the state. Many wild animals make their homes in the trees. Oaks also provide food for a variety of Iowa's animals. Residents have long used oak to make products such as furniture.

IOWA

⭐ Capital City: **Des Moines**

Des Moines was founded in 1843. It covers an area just over 80 square miles (207 square kilometers) and has a population of 203,433 people and growing. Des Moines became the capital of Iowa in 1857. Des Moines is a center of culture in Iowa, with history and art museums, a botanical garden and zoo, a symphony, and many performing arts groups.

⭐ Highest Point: **Hawkeye Point**

Iowa's highest point lies just 3.5 miles (5.6 kilometers) from the state's northern border with Minnesota. Hawkeye Point reaches 1,670 feet (510 meters). Hawkeye Point features an information kiosk, granite markers, and signs pointing to the highest points in the other forty-nine states. The high ground lies 100 feet (30 m) south of an old silo.

⭐ State Rock: **Geode**

Geodes are hard-shelled rocks with mineral crystals inside. Many of these rocks are found in limestone formations throughout Iowa. The crystals inside the geodes were formed over thousands of years as water dripped on the limestone. One of the most productive and famous collecting regions is within a 35-mile (56 km) radius of Keokuk, Iowa.

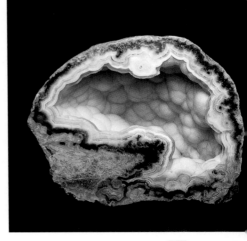

Population Data: US Bureau of the Census, 2010

Rolling hills of rich topsoil make
Iowa a perfect place for farming.

The Hawkeye State

People often think of Iowa as a flatland covered with many farms devoted to raising corn, soybeans, cattle, chicken, and hogs. That is an accurate description, but it is not complete. While it is true that 90 percent of the state's land is farmland, Iowa also has areas of rolling hills, towering **bluffs**, valleys, forests, rivers, and lakes. The landscape is also dotted with cities, towns, and villages.

In a number of ways, Iowa is a state that is in the middle. In geographic terms, for example, the state is in the middle of the United States. The Mississippi River, which forms Iowa's eastern border, divides the nation into east and west.

Iowa is also in a middle position in terms of size and population. The state covers a land area of 55,857 square miles (144,669 sq km), making it twenty-third in size when it is compared to all the other states. In population, Iowa has more than three million people. This means that on average, there are 54.5 people for every 1 square mile (2.6 sq km) in the state. This is called the population density. Thirty-four states have a higher population density than Iowa, and fifteen have a lower population density.

Most of Iowa is covered by farms that produce crops such as corn, soybeans, and hay.

The Land

Tens of thousands of years ago, the land that now includes Iowa was shaped by an Ice Age, or a period when **glaciers**, or great sheets of ice, slowly moved down over much of the continent. The moving glaciers created lakes, leveled hills, and pushed around massive amounts of soil and rock. These giant glaciers are the reason why Iowa can be divided into three geographic regions.

The northeastern region of what is now Iowa was covered by only one glacier, so it was not affected by the force of the ice as much as the rest of the state was. The central region, which covers more than half of the state's area, is the most level region. There, the melting glacier left behind deep, rich soil. The third region, which makes up the western and southern fringes of present-day Iowa, has soil that was blown so hard and for so long by the winds that it was turned into hills and ridges called Loess Hills.

Iowa Borders	
North:	Minnesota
South:	Missouri
	Illinois
East:	Mississippi River
	Wisconsin
	Illinois
West:	Missouri River
	Nebraska
	South Dakota

The forests of northeastern Iowa are a great place to see the colors of fall.

Northeastern Iowa

Visitors who enter Iowa through the northeastern corner might be surprised to see a landscape that has more hills and forests than flat cornfields and hog farms. Bordered by the majestic span of the Mississippi River, this northeastern land also has river valleys and wooded hills of oak, maple, elm, and other trees. In the fall, these wooded areas sport reds, oranges, and yellows as the leaves change colors.

This part of Iowa also has sections of rugged hills and bluffs that rise 300 to 400 feet (91–122 m) above the Mississippi. Wildlife and fish **refuges** dot the river area. The river valley is also part of the Mississippi Flyway—the great migration route for birds moving north in summer and south in winter. Enormous flocks of Canada geese, snow geese, ducks, and other birds flap to noisy landings in Iowa's protected areas along the river.

Many communities such as Bellevue grew along the Mississippi River.

IOWA
COUNTY MAP

Adair	7,682	Boone	26,306	Cass	13,956
Adams	4,029	Bremer	24,276	Cedar	18,499
Allamakee	14,330	Buchanan	20,958	Cerro Gordo	44,151
Appanoose	12,887	Buena Vista	20,260	Cherokee	12,072
Audubon	6,119	Butler	14,867	Chickasaw	12,439
Benton	26,076	Calhoun	9,670	Clarke	9,286
Black Hawk	131,090	Carroll	20,816	Clay	16,667

IOWA

POPULATION BY COUNTY

County	Population	County	Population	County	Population
Clayton	18,129	Jackson	19,848	Pocahontas	7,310
Clinton	49,116	Jasper	36,842	Polk	430,635
Crawford	17,096	Jefferson	16,843	Pottawattamie	93,149
Dallas	66,137	Johnson	130,882	Poweshiek	18,914
Davis	8,753	Jones	20,638	Ringgold	5,131
Decatur	8,457	Keokuk	10,511	Sac	10,350
Delaware	17,764	Kossuth	15,543	Scott	165,224
Des Moines	40,325	Lee	35,862	Shelby	12,167
Dickinson	16,667	Linn	211,226	Sioux	33,704
Dubuque	93,653	Louisa	11,387	Story	89,542
Emmet	10,302	Lucas	8,898	Tama	17,767
Fayette	20,880	Lyon	11,581	Taylor	6,317
Floyd	16,303	Madison	15,679	Union	12,534
Franklin	10,680	Mahaska	22,381	Van Buren	7,570
Fremont	7,441	Marion	33,309	Wapello	35,625
Greene	9,337	Marshall	40,648	Warren	46,228
Grundy	12,453	Mills	15,059	Washington	21,704
Guthrie	10,954	Mitchell	10,772	Wayne	6,403
Hamilton	15,673	Monona	9,243	Webster	38,013
Hancock	11,341	Monroe	7,970	Winnebago	10,866
Hardin	17,534	Montgomery	10,740	Winneshiek	21,058
Harrison	14,937	Muscatine	42,747	Woodbury	102,177
Henry	20,145	O'Brien	14,398	Worth	7,598
Howard	9,566	Osceola	6,462	Wright	13,229
Humboldt	9,814	Page	15,943		
Ida	7,089	Palo Alto	9,421		
Iowa	16,355	Plymouth	24,981		

Source: US Bureau of the Census, 2010

Long, winding rivers, which rise in the prairie lands of central Iowa, flow in a southeasterly direction into the Mississippi River. Several of these rivers carve deep gorges as they near the Mississippi.

North-Central Iowa

The glaciers that moved south into the north-central area of Iowa produced a flat landscape that creates the picture of Iowa as a land of endless cornfields. The deep soil deposited by the retreating ice sheet is said to be among the most fertile soil in the world. This makes it perfect for growing crops.

This landscape is part of the Great Plains region of North America. These plains extend from Iowa to the Rocky Mountains a couple of states away. Until the late 1800s, great herds of bison roamed this prairie land, moving north from Mexico to Canada. As pioneer settlers from the East and from Europe moved to the prairie, the wild grassland was replaced with wheat and corn crops. Wild bison herds disappeared due to hunting and loss of natural grazing land. The Great Plains eventually became the place where the world's largest supply of grain was produced.

A ridge that runs across this region of Iowa—from northwest to southeast—is called the Missouri-Mississippi Divide. Rivers on the west of the divide flow west into the Missouri River. Rivers on the east flow southeast into the Mississippi River. The longest of Iowa's rivers, the Des Moines River, flows 485 miles (781 km) through the center of the state. The state capital, Des Moines, which is also Iowa's largest city, is located on both banks of the Des Moines River.

Western and Southern Iowa

Wrapped around the north-central region of Iowa to the west is the third region, which geologists call the Dissected Till Plains. The first of the four great ice sheets that once covered Iowa left behind huge quantities of till, or layers of soil and rocks. Over thousands of years, after the ice sheet had disappeared, streams cut through, or dissected, the plains. Glacial movement over time also created bodies of water.

The wind also helped to shape this region. Wind pushed soil up against the Missouri River, forming bluffs that rise 100 to 300 feet (30–91 m) above the river. The soil here is deeper than anywhere else in the world, except for a river valley in China. These types of land formations are called **loess** hills. Loess is lose, yellow-gray sediment that is blown and deposited by the wind. Because of years of wind and water moving around the soil and

The wind molded hills of loess that cover large parts of Iowa.

land, Iowa's loess hills are rough, jagged, and strangely shaped in some places. There are stair-like landforms and even some that look like parts of an animal's body.

The northwestern parts of the state are also home to a number of small lakes. Larger lakes, such as Storm Lake, are popular spots for fishing, boating, and other water sports. Major cities in western Iowa include Council Bluffs and Sioux City.

Climate

Iowa has a continental climate, which is a climate that is found in the interior of Earth's different continents. More simply, a continental climate has cold winters and warm, humid summers. However, there are variations in climate within the state. For instance, the northwest has cold January winters, with an average temperature of 14 degrees Fahrenheit (–10 degrees Celsius). In the southeast, though, the average January temperature is 22°F (–5.5°C).

At times in Iowa's history, the temperatures have strayed far from their averages. The highest recorded temperature in Iowa occurred on July 20, 1934, when it hit 118°F (47.7°C) in the city of Keokuk. The lowest temperature ever recorded was on January 12, 1912, when it dropped to a freezing –47°F (–43.8°C) in the city of Washta.

Throughout the state, warm July days have an average temperature of 74°F (23°C). The state also gets a good deal of rainfall in the summer. Precipitation, which takes the form of rain when it is warm and snow, sleet, or freezing rain when it is cold, is usually four times greater in June than in the winter months. Rain also varies according to different regions.

★ 10 ★ KEY SITES ★ ★

Fenelon Place Elevator

Field of Dreams

Grotto of the Redemption

1. Capitol Building

The Capitol Building is located in Iowa's capital city of Des Moines. The Capitol is a living museum and international cultural facility. The World Food Prize Laureate Award Ceremony is held there every October.

2. Fenelon Place Elevator

This 296-foot (90 m) elevator is located in Dubuque. It claims to be the shortest and steepest railroad in the world. From the upper observation deck, there are views of Iowa, Illinois and Wisconsin. It is listed in the National Register of Historic Places.

3. Field of Dreams

The Field of Dreams is a baseball field that was the setting for the movie of the same name. The field is located in Dyersville and has souvenir shops. Visitors can even run the bases of the baseball diamond.

4. Grotto of the Redemption

The **grotto** is a religious shrine in West Bend. Nine grottos, or caverns, depict scenes in the life of Jesus. It is believed to hold the largest collection of minerals, fossils, shells, and **petrifications** in one place.

5. High Trestle Trail

The High Trestle Trail runs for 25 miles (40 km) from Ankeny to Woodward. It is estimated that three thousand people use this trail every week. The trestle bridge provides views of the Des Moines River Valley.

IOWA ★ ★ ★ ★ ★ ★

6. Iowa 80 Trucking Museum

Antique trucks are on display at this museum in Walcott. Exhibits include the Antique Truck of the Month and Antique Toy Trucks. Visitors can watch short films about trucking history. Teachers can plan field trips to this museum.

7. National Mississippi River Museum & Aquarium

This museum and aquarium are located in Dubuque. The museum features exhibits on the culture and history of America's rivers. The aquarium is home to wildlife that is often found in the Mississippi River basin.

8. National Motorcycle Museum

This museum in Anamosa has a collection of motorcycles. Some of the motorcycles, photos, postcards, and posters are more than one hundred years old. The bikes come from all over the world, including ones from Japan and England.

9. Pikes Peak State Park

Pikes Peak State Park, which includes the Effigy Mounds National Monument, is near McGregor. Visitors can see views of the Wisconsin and Mississippi Rivers from a 500-foot (152 m) bluff. Hiking, camping, and picnicking are available.

10. Reiman Gardens

These 17-acre (7 ha) gardens are located on the Iowa State University campus. There are several garden areas depending on the season, an indoor butterfly wing, and several greenhouses. Works of art and beautiful architecture are also housed here.

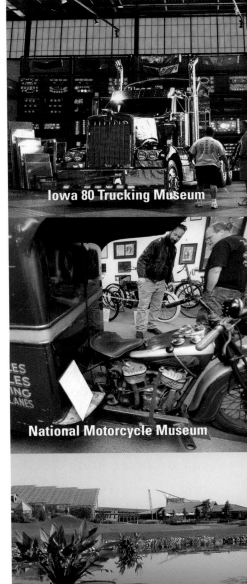

Iowa 80 Trucking Museum

National Motorcycle Museum

Reiman Gardens

Warm summers make Iowa's lakes popular places to relax.

Each year, the northwest gets about 28 inches (71 centimeters) compared to the southeast's 35 inches (89 cm). Snowfall shows a similar difference, with an average of 50 inches (127 cm) of snow per year in the north compared to 22 inches (56 cm) a year in southern Iowa.

Weather changes can occur rapidly, and even Iowans are sometimes surprised by sudden changes. Sometimes the temperature can rise or fall many degrees in a day. A burst of cold air from the northwest can cause a sudden drop in temperature, while warm air can bring a sudden blast of hot air along with heavy thunderstorms.

One example of a month when severe weather changes occurred took place in May 2013, when a snowstorm swept across the north-central United States. The storm was called Winter Storm Achilles. Eleven inches (28 cm) of snow fell in parts of Iowa, which broke the record for the most snowfall in May. Just a couple of weeks later, summer was under way. Temperatures reached over 100°F (37.7°C) in some parts of the state.

Wildlife

In the early years of settlement by pioneers from the East and from Europe, the newcomers stayed in the eastern region of the state. There, the forests provided lumber for homes, while the rivers were used for water and transportation. During this time, the settlers and their descendants cut down many of the forests.

In spite of so much woodland being destroyed, Iowa still has about 1,500,000 acres (607,028 hectares) of forest. Hardwood trees, such as maple, oak, hickory, and walnut, grow

Prairie trillium is one of the many kinds of flowers that decorate Iowa.

in the river valleys. The hardwoods not only produce the spectacular colors of autumn, but also provide homes and food for Iowa wildlife. They are also used for fine furniture. Evergreens, such as white fir, white and Norway spruce, and red and jack pines, are common in the state. Red cedar, one of the only evergreens native to Iowa, is found along the Cedar River. Farther west, cottonwoods and willows are fairly common along the rivers.

An attractive sight in the spring is the burst of wildflowers that blanket Iowa's prairie grasslands. From March to October, Iowa's roadsides also have colorful blossoms. The blooming display begins with violets, marsh marigolds, and bloodroots. Summer flowers include prairie lilies, purple phlox, and wild roses. Autumn is the time for prairie asters, goldenrod, sunflowers, and gentians.

Many migrating birds like to build their nests in fields, rather than in trees. The open farmlands of Iowa provide excellent nesting grounds. Quail, partridge, and pheasant have plenty of grain to feed on as they nest among the corn, hay, or oats. An Iowa state hatchery in Boone County raises these species to be released into the wild as game birds, which are birds designated to be hunted. Enormous flocks of winter fowl—ducks and geese—cross Iowa by either the Missouri River or the Mississippi Flyway.

White-tailed deer are still plentiful in the state, as are coyotes, foxes, and opossums. Smaller animals like rabbits, squirrels, and chipmunks are common in wooded areas. Fast-moving streams are well stocked with bass and trout. Lakes and slower streams contain fish such as largemouth bass, bluegills, crappies, catfish, northern pike, and walleyes.

Iowa's farmers create habitat that can shelter and feed pheasants.

Restoring the Environment

Many Iowans have long been concerned about the state's land, water, and wildlife. In the mid-twentieth century, a large number of Iowans decided that they were not pleased with what was happening to the state's natural environment. At that time the state did not have the really bad air or water **pollution** of some US cities. There were other problems, though, such as the loss of natural tallgrass prairies and habitats for wildlife.

Iowans found ways to make changes. South of Des Moines, for example, local and state agencies pressured the federal government to establish the Neal Smith National Wildlife Refuge. More than 5,000 acres (2,023 ha) were set aside to restore prairie to what it looked like around 150 years ago. Thanks to these efforts, tall prairie grasses once again bend in the steady breeze, and many types of wildflowers provide brilliant splashes of color. Small groups of wild bison have been reintroduced to the prairie, along with other animals and birds that were once common prairie residents. The Prairie Learning Center gives visitors a chance to learn more about Iowa's prairies. As more farmland is purchased, the refuge continues to grow.

Another responsibility of the Neal Smith National Wildlife Refuge is to track the bison herds. The refuge keeps track of the size of bison herds and removes bison when a herd grows too large. Millions of bison, or buffalo, once lived on the prairie. Visitors to the refuge are able to take an auto tour through enclosures were bison and elk live.

Other small wildlife preserves are scattered throughout Iowa, including several that form part of the Upper Mississippi River National Wildlife and Fish Refuge. The Hayden

Prairie State Preserve, near Chester, covers only 242 acres (98 ha), but it has around one hundred different species of wildflower.

Northeastern Iowa has Red Cedar Woodland in Muscatine County. This preserve is a protected area that is part of a large island in the Cedar River. It can only be reached by boat, so the woodland is a perfect place for plants such as maples and sycamores and birds such as bald eagles and hawks to live and grow undisturbed.

In Their Own Words

"There's a lot to be proud about in Iowa."
—Sharon Rexroth, author of *Iowa from the Sky*

In another part of the state, the people of Albia, Iowa, faced a different environmental problem. As coal mining became less popular in the region, many buildings were abandoned. Victorian buildings, which had once been elegant, had fallen into disrepair. They were covered with coal dust and grime. Some newspapers called Albia the "ugliest town in Iowa."

In 1970, Albians launched Operation Facelift. Buildings were restored and painted. Businesses were drawn to the area because of low rents and because there were so many skilled workers living in Albia. Within a decade, Albia became a model for restoring a community. In 1985, the efforts of Albia's residents were recognized. The entire downtown area, including more than ninety Victorian structures, was added to the National Register of Historic Places.

From the state's beautiful wildlife and natural scenery to its historic buildings, Iowans are dedicated to protecting the Hawkeye State.

Refuges protect wildlife and give people a chance to learn more about the birds and other animals that live in the state.

Bald Eagle

Eastern Red Cedar

Elk

1. Bald Eagle

In the past, the populations of bald eagles were shrinking due to pollution, overhunting, and habitat destruction. Laws and wildlife programs have helped to protect these eagles. In Keokuk, shuttle buses take bird watchers to observation areas where they can see these birds.

2. Canada Goose

Females weigh an average of 11 pounds (5 kilograms) and the males 12 pounds (5.5 kg). Draining of wetlands and hunting wiped out the birds in Iowa by 1900. They were reintroduced in 1964. Nesting in Iowa runs from mid-March to mid-April.

3. Eastern Red Cedar

The eastern red cedar grows in all parts of the state. In the wild, the trees provide homes for animals. People often plant these cedars to block the wind or to keep soil in certain areas from washing away.

4. Elk

Millions of elk once roamed Iowa's prairies, eating grasses and other plants. Today, the Neal Smith National Wildlife Refuge maintains a herd of elk within a 700-acre (283 ha) enclosure. Elk are important to the prairie ecosystem.

5. Muskrat

These large rodents are common in and around Iowa's lakes and ponds. With their brown fur and their heavy 12-inch (30.5 cm) tails, muskrats are often mistaken for beavers. Muskrats spend much of their time in the water.

6. Peregrine Falcon

These birds of prey can fly up to 60 miles per hour (96.5 kilometers per hour). When they dive, they can reach speeds of up to 260 miles per hour (418 kmh). Historically, peregrine falcons nested on cliffs along the Mississippi and Cedar Rivers.

7. Prairie Grasses

The western two-thirds of Iowa were once covered with a variety of grasses. Some of these grasses ranged in height from 1 foot to 7 feet (0.3–2 m). The prairie grasses provide homes and food for many kinds of wildlife.

8. Seedheads of Big Bluestem

These grasses can grow to 8 feet (2.4 m) tall during warm seasons. Their presence in Iowa fields boosts wildlife and saves soil. These types of grass are known to survive in heat and droughts.

9. Trumpeter Swan

Hunting and loss of habitat nearly wiped out trumpeter swans in Iowa. This native bird was reintroduced in Iowa in pinioned pairs in the early 1990s. Pinioned means their wings are clipped so they can't fly. Wild offspring of these pinioned pairs are repopulating trumpeter swans in Iowa.

10. White-Tailed Deer

These deer were abundant throughout Iowa when settlers arrived in the 1800s. Their population has gone up and down due to clearing of the land and hunting. There are an estimated two hundred thousand in the state.

Peregrine Falcon

Seedheads of Big Bluestem

Trumpeter Swan

The Julien Dubuque Monument honors the trader whose settlement became the city of Dubuque on the Mississippi River.

From the Beginning

The first humans moved into the region that now includes Iowa about twelve thousand years ago, as the last of the giant glaciers retreated. These early native people lived by gathering wild foods and hunting.

About three thousand years ago, the **ancestors** of modern Native Americans learned to grow crops. This provided a more reliable food supply and also allowed them to live in settled communities. They did not have to follow herds of wild animals or move south during the winter months to find wild plants and other sources of food.

Also around this time, there was another remarkable development. Early Native American people started to build large ceremonial mounds. Some of these mounds measured 130 feet (40 m) long and up to 70 feet (21 m) wide. The mounds were used for both burials and for religious ceremonies. Many mounds were built in the shape of animals such as birds and bears. A few of the mounds resembled human forms.

At one time, an estimated ten thousand of these mounds were spread through the middle of North America. The groups of people who built these mounds were part of the Hopewell tradition. Artifacts found in the mounds have been examined by scientists. They believe that the early people who lived in the area of Iowa may have traded with different

Effigy Mounds National Monument, which is near Marquette, is made up of about two hundred mounds.

Natives living around the Rocky Mountains to the west, the Atlantic coast to the east, along the Great Lakes to the north, and near the Gulf of Mexico in the south. As pioneer settlers cleared the land for farming, they destroyed all but about two hundred of these mounds. Those that remain in Iowa are carefully protected, and only scientists are allowed to search the mounds.

About seven hundred years ago, the Hopewell people vanished. No one knows for certain what happened to them. It is possible that they moved to other parts of the continent or were driven out by other groups of people. All that remains today are their amazing mounds.

In the years that followed, other Native groups made their homes in the region. The Ioway (or Iowa) and the Omaha settled in the northwestern part of the state by the Big Sioux River. The Oto, the Missouri, the Sioux, the Illiniwek (or Illinois), and the Ottawa also lived and hunted in the land that includes present-day Iowa. Other groups also came to this area, including the Sac (or Sauk) and the Fox. The Fox were also called the Meskwaki or Mesquakie.

Native Americans provided food for their families by farming, hunting, and gathering wild foods. As farmers, they built villages and planted crops such as corn, beans, and squash. As hunters and gatherers, the Natives traveled in the summer months on long

Native Americans lived near the region's rivers and traveled long distances by canoe to trade with other tribes.

hunting trips and lived in portable homes, such as tepees, as they searched for deer, elk, and bison.

There were, at one time, so many Native groups living in the region that fights broke out over who could live there and who had the right to hunt. Other types of wars were fought among Native Americans because some groups were enemies of other groups. This caused some Natives to be forced out of the area, usually moving farther west. The Ioway people were one of these groups.

New Arrivals

In the 1600s, white settlers began to visit the region that now includes Iowa. Two of the first were the French explorers Louis Jolliet and Father Jacques Marquette, who traveled down the Mississippi River by canoe in 1673. Jolliet and Marquette were searching for a river passageway that traveled from the East to the Pacific Ocean in the West. They most likely did not stay for very long in the land that includes present-day Iowa. However, they did take note of some of the Native cultures and the wildlife found on Iowa's shores of the Mississippi River.

In Their Own Words

"In seed time, learn. In harvest, teach. In winter, enjoy."
–William Blake, poet

The Native People

When settlers arrived in Iowa, there were five tribes already there. These five tribes were the Ioway, the Dakota Sioux, the Illiniwek or Illinois, the Missouri, and the Oto. The Ioway tribe covered more than half the state, primarily in the central and southern areas. The Dakota Sioux were in the north. The Illiniwek were in the east. The Oto and Missouri inhabited a small portion of the southwest corner. The state name came from the Ioway tribe. "Iowa" is a Siouan word meaning "sleepy ones." As the white settlers began taking over Native American land, more tribes came to Iowa. These included the Sac and Fox Tribe of the Mississippi, also known as the Meskwaki.

Most of the Native Americans throughout the state would have spoken similar languages, but different dialects. A dialect refers to a special variety of the same language. The Dakota, Ioway, Missouri, and Oto all spoke versions of the Siouan language. The Illiniwek spoke an Algonquian language. The Meskwaki, who arrived later, spoke an Iroquoian language. These groups lived in villages in fixed homes, not tepees. They traveled on the rivers in canoes made from hollowed out logs.

Like the Native Americans in many other states, those in Iowa were not met kindly by the white settlers. The Europeans who had come to America wanted to take over the land and claim it for themselves. Many of the Native tribes were nearly wiped out by war, and the survivors were sent to live in Kansas and Oklahoma. Their land was taken over by white settlers.

These three chiefs once guided tribes that lived in the region that became Iowa.

The Sac and Fox Tribe of the Mississippi, or Meskwaki, is the only federally recognized tribe that remains in Iowa. Members of this tribe live on a settlement in Central Iowa. There are approximately 1,400 enrolled tribal members remaining. The Meskwaki Nation owns 8,000 acres (3,237 ha) of land in Tama County and Palo Alto County. The Meskwaki Nation purchased the land on July 13, 1857. They recognize this day to remember the foresight of their leaders who purchased the land. They also celebrate having a home to grow crops, raise children, and practice their religion without outside interference.

Spotlight on the Meskwaki

"Meskwaki" is pronounced "mesk-wah-kee." It is sometimes spelled "Mesquakie" or "Mesquaki." The name means "red earth people."

Distribution: The Meskwaki originally occupied eastern woodlands and prairie regions in Michigan and Wisconsin. Today, most of the Meskwaki live on reservations in Iowa, Oklahoma, and Kansas.

Homes: The Meskwaki were known for two types of dwellings: wigwams and lodges. Wigwams are dome-shaped houses. Their lodges were rectangular and covered with bark. Today, most Meskwaki build wigwams or lodges for ritual purposes, but they live in modern houses or apartments.

Food: The Meskwaki were farming people. Women grew corn, beans, and squash. The men hunted deer, small game, and sometimes buffalo. The Meskwaki also were known to eat berries, fruit, honey, cornbread, and soups.

Clothing: Meskwaki women wore wraparound skirts, and Meskwaki men wore breechcloths and leggings. Shirts were not necessary in the Meskwaki culture. They wore ponchos when the weather was cool. On their feet, the Meskwaki wore mocassins. Meskwaki men also wore caps made of otter fur. Women wore their hair in long braids or in a bun gathered behind their neck. Meskwaki warriors often wore their hair in the Mohawk style or shaved their heads except for a scalp lock.

Art: Meskwaki women traditionally made dolls for their daughters out of cornhusks. Meskwaki artists were also known for their quill embroidery, pottery, and beadwork.

Explorers Jacques Marquette and Louis Jolliet explored the Mississippi River and kept good relations with the Native Americans they met.

In 1682, another French explorer called René-Robert Cavalier, sieur de La Salle traveled down the Mississippi. As La Salle traveled down the river, he claimed all the land—which stretched from Canada to the Gulf of Mexico—on both sides of the river for France. The land was called the Louisiana Territory, in honor of France's king, Louis XIV.

In the years that followed, fur traders from the French colonies in Canada also traveled through the region that would become Iowa. They traded with the different Native American groups that they came across, but they did not establish any permanent settlements. As more European explorers and settlers came to the area, they brought modern goods for the natives to use. The Native Americans traded for guns and the tame horses the Europeans brought with them.

During most of the 1700s, the French Canadians and the Native Americans got along well. For example, the Natives of the region had found ways to mine lead. French-Canadian traders who were on good terms with the Natives, men such as Julien Dubuque, also took part in the lead mining. In 1788, Dubuque began to establish a very profitable mining site and settlement. Besides providing lead, Dubuque's industry increased

Chief Black Hawk

Iowa is called "The Hawkeye State" to honor Chief Black Hawk. Chief Black Hawk led a battle against the white settlers to try to protect the Native Americans' land. He became the first Native American to have his autobiography published in the United States.

trade to the region, bringing in goods from the East and other places. The city of Dubuque is named for this early settler.

A New Country

In the late 1700s, another drama was occurring far to the east. Great Britain had earlier established thirteen colonies along the Atlantic coast of North America. By the late 1700s, there were nearly three million people living in those colonies. In 1776, the colonies declared their independence from the British. When the American Revolution ended in 1783, the colonies became the independent country of the United States of America.

In 1803, France agreed to sell the Louisiana Territory (which included the area that would later become Iowa) to the United States for about $15 million, which would be over $230 million in today's dollars. When the new government bought this land from France, the size of the United States nearly doubled. This land deal was called the Louisiana Purchase. Explorers Meriwether Lewis and William Clark worked for the US government, searching for a water route from the Mississippi River and up the Missouri River to the Columbia River, which flowed into the Pacific Ocean. Their explorations took them through the Louisiana Territory. Between 1804 and 1806, the Lewis and Clark **expedition** explored the land that stretched from the Mississippi River, through present-day Iowa, and then even further to the west, almost to the Pacific Ocean. Lewis and Clark would eventually extend their search to the West Coast, ending their travels at the Pacific coast of Oregon. As they explored these lands, they took note of the different types of animals and plants and the Native cultures they encountered. They also found that the Missouri and Columbia Rivers don't connect.

One of the most amazing aspects of the Lewis and Clark expedition was their ability to survive hardship and danger. Fifty-six men traveled through the unmapped wilderness for nearly three years. During their travels, they encountered nearly thirty different Native American groups that spoke

The Sergeant Floyd Monument in Sioux City honors the only person to have died on the Lewis and Clark expedition.

Making a Coffee Filter Wild Rose

What You Need

Coffee filters

Food Coloring

A dish

Scissors

Green pipe cleaner

Wax paper

Tape

Stapler

What To Do

- Stack two sets of three filters and flatten them. Each flower requires six filters.
- Place some water in the dish and add food coloring until you get the shade you want.
- Fold a stack of filters so the pleated sides remain on top.
- Holding the center of the filters, dip them into the water until the colors cover at least half of the filters.
- Unfold the filters and lay them on the wax paper. Repeat with the second stack of filters. Leave them all to dry, from half an hour to overnight.
- When dry, take one stack of filters and fold them in half, and then in half again. Cut scallops across the top edge. Fold the second stack the same way and cut scallops so this stack is shorter than the first stack.

- Lay the shorter stack on top of the other stack and refold them all. Pinch the bottom and staple it.
- Flatten the stapled filters and, one by one, fluff them to the center to look like petals.
- Staple a pipe cleaner to the base, then wrap the stapled part with tape.
- Repeat with different colors and you can make a beautiful bouquet.

many different languages. They also faced bone-chilling weather conditions, rugged mountains, and losses of supplies, and yet only one man died during this expedition. Sergeant Charles Floyd died of problems caused by an inflamed appendix, a small organ attached to the gut. Floyd was buried near present-day Sioux City, and today a 100-foot-tall (30.5 m) monument marks his grave.

A Clash of Cultures

In the early 1800s, the United States began to grow and to expand with startling speed. Pioneer families pushed westward, hungry for the promise of land. They soon crossed the Mississippi River and started buying land from Native Americans when they could. When the Native American people were not willing to sell their land, the settlers often fought with them. In many cases, they forced the Natives off of the land. Many of the Native Americans throughout the Midwest felt the pressure of the westward movement of settlers onto their land.

In 1804, representatives of the Sac and Fox tribes signed a treaty that ceded—or gave away—all of their territory east of the Mississippi River. Chief Black Hawk, a Sac chief, tried to claim the treaty was invalid. Years later, Black Hawk himself signed the treaty. However, he later claimed that he didn't know that would mean he would have to move from his home village.

Some groups or tribes moved farther west to get away from the white settlers who were moving in from the East. In 1831, the US government ordered the Sac and Fox tribes—who were then living in what would become Illinois—to move into the area that would become Iowa. Black Hawk did not want to move his people. He wanted to reclaim his homeland. To do this, he brought together many warriors and organized an uprising in 1832. After seeing the number of US soldiers, Black Hawk tried to surrender. The US soldiers were confused by his gesture, however, and one of his truce bearers was killed. This began the Black Hawk War.

In Their Own Words

"Corn can add inches in a single day; if you listened, you could hear it grow."
–Laura Ruby, author

Black Hawk and his men won a significant victory in May, but the US troops were relentless. The war lasted fifteen weeks and the losses were lopsided. Approximately 70 settlers or soldiers were killed, but between 450 and 600 Native Americans lost their lives. Chief Black Hawk was captured and

The St. Paul and Sioux City R.R. Co.

ARE OFFERING THEIR

CHOICE LANDS in

South-western Minnesota and North-western Iowa,

at prices ranging from $4 to $6 per acre, on the most favorable terms.

These lands are acknowledged to be superior to any in the North-west, being in the great Wheat Belt, the crops of Corn, Sorghum, Flax, Hemp, Barley, Rye, and Oats, are very prolific.

No section of the N. W. offers lands so well adapted for STOCK RAISING and DAIRY purposes, being celebrated for its superior Grasses and well watered by Lakes and Streams. Climate unsurpassed. For Maps and Pamphlets giving full particulars, address

Land Department St. Paul & Sioux City R.R. Co., St. Paul, Minn.

Settlers were attracted to Iowa by advertisements posted by railroad companies promising rich farmland.

jailed in Virginia. Later, the Americans brought him on a tour to other tribes around the country. The idea was to show other Native American chiefs that it was of no use to fight against the might of the United States because the tribes were sure to lose.

Because he lost this war, Chief Black Hawk agreed to give a strip of land 50 miles (80.5 km) wide along the Mississippi River to the US government. He hoped this land, known as the Black Hawk Purchase, would satisfy the settlers' hunger for land. Settlers rapidly moved to this land, and in 1834, it became part of the Michigan Territory. Westward settlement by the whites continued.

The Ioway Tribe

The state of Iowa got its name from the Ioway Tribe. The Ioway Tribe represented some of the first people to inhabit present-day Iowa. Pronounced "eye-oh-way," the tribe name

Hundreds of Sac and Fox warriors were killed crossing the Mississippi River in the Battle of Bad Axe, the final one of the Black Hawk War.

comes from the Sioux word meaning "sleepy ones." However, the Ioway called themselves Baxoje, which means "gray snow." In addition to the land of present-day Iowa, the Ioway also lived in southwestern Minnesota.

As white settlers moved west, many Native American tribes were forced to move. This included the Ioway. The Ioway were forced to move to **reservations** in Kansas, Nebraska, and Oklahoma. Most of the Ioway still alive today live in these states. The Ioway in Kansas and Nebraska live on a reservation. The Ioways in Oklahoma live on trust lands.

Over time, the Ioway have grown more accustomed to the ways of the white settlers. For example, most of them speak English today. In the past, Ioway spoke the Chiewere language. Very few people still speak this language, though some younger Ioway are working to learn this ancient language. A simple greeting used between men and boys is "aho" (pronounced ah-hoe). Women and girls may say "aha" (pronounced ah-hah).

Ioway men and women had different roles from each other. Ioway men hunted and protected the tribe, going to war when necessary. Only Ioway men were chiefs. Ioway women were in charge of farming, childcare, and cooking. Both men and women took part in storytelling, artwork, music, and traditional medicine.

10 KEY CITIES

1. Des Moines: 203,433

Des Moines is both the largest city and the capital of Iowa. Iowa is home to the first caucuses of the presidential primary, so many presidential candidates set up their campaign headquarters in Des Moines.

2. Cedar Rapids: 126,326

Cedar Rapids is a center for arts and culture, and there are seventy-four parks or recreational facilities there. Cedar Rapids is nicknamed the "City of Five Seasons" because short commutes to work give residents more time to enjoy life, or a fifth season.

3. Davenport: 99,685

Davenport is located halfway between Chicago, Illinois, and Des Moines, Iowa. Davenport is known for frequent flooding since it is located on the Mississippi River. The first chiropractic adjustment took place in Davenport.

4. Sioux City: 82,684

Sioux City is located in northwest Iowa on the Missouri River. Sioux City has been recognized by national magazines for several reasons. Sioux City has been ranked one of the best places to live and one of the best places for small businesses.

5. Waterloo: 68,406

Waterloo was originally named Prairie Rapids Crossing until the opening of its first office. Waterloo has a humid continental climate. The city is home to the National Wrestling Hall of Fame Dan Gable Museum and the Sullivan Brothers Iowa Veterans Museum (*left*).

Des Moines

Waterloo

IOWA ★ ★ ★ ★ ★

6. Iowa City: 67,862

Iowa City was recognized as the only City of Literature in North or South America. The University of Iowa, which hosts the Iowa Writers' Workshop, employs more than a third of the residents of Iowa City.

7. Council Bluffs: 62,230

Council Bluffs used to be known as Kanesville. This was the starting point of the Mormon Trail, which was traveled by members of the Church of Jesus Christ of Latter-day Saints as they headed to Utah. Council Bluffs is right across the Missouri River from Omaha, Nebraska.

8. Ames: 58,965

Ames is the birthplace of the Atanasoff-Berry, the world's first electronic digital computer. The Iowa State University of Science and Technology is in Ames. The university is a research institution.

9. Dubuque: 57,637

Dubuque has a unique location at the junction of Iowa, Illinois, and Wisconsin. It is one of the few large cities in Iowa that has hills. Dubuque was long known for manufacturing. Its economy now includes health care, education, tourism, and publishing.

10. West Des Moines: 56,609

West Des Moines was home to the Sac and Fox tribes until 1845. The area then became known as Valley Junction, which is now a collection of historic shops and restaurants that links the past to the present.

Ames

Dubuque

Avon Public Library

Iowa Becomes a State

Before 1838, Iowa had been a part of the Wisconsin Territory. In 1838, the Iowa Territory was established. Robert Lucas was appointed as the first governor. In 1839, the territorial capital was built in Iowa City. The population continued to grow.

By 1846, more than one hundred thousand white settlers lived in Iowa. On December 28, 1846, Iowa was admitted to the Union as the twenty-ninth state. Iowa City was the state's capital. In 1857, however, the capital was moved to Des Moines. This was because Des Moines was closer to the center of the state.

During the 1850s, Iowa continued to grow at a quick pace as word spread of the state's rich soil. Farmers knew that such good soil meant that crops would be successful and profitable. By 1860, more than 650,000 people lived in the state. Most of the settlers chose land in eastern Iowa and along river valleys in the western region of Iowa. They chose these locations because the forests in these areas provided plenty of wood for building homes, barns, and fences. The many rivers also provided transportation and waterpower for mills, which were used to grind corn and other grains. Settlers avoided

The first capitol built in the state is now on the campus of the University of Iowa in Iowa City.

the Great Plains area in the central and western regions of the state because the grassland had few trees and the land did not look like it could be farmed. The sod, or soil made up of centuries of matted, tangled grasses, seemed too thick for a plow to cut through. As a result, the settlers pressed rapidly across the grasslands, heading for fertile lands in Oregon and California.

Pioneer families in Iowa grew corn, wheat, and oats. Corn, which was used primarily to feed livestock, soon became the major crop. Farmers also raised cattle, chickens, and hogs. Towns were established along the rivers because of the ease of transportation. Most of the state's cities, including Des Moines, Cedar Rapids, Davenport, Iowa City, and Dubuque, began this way.

The period from the 1840s to 1860 was Iowa's frontier days. Law and order were established slowly in some of the western towns. This made it a dangerous place to live, but many brave settlers pushed through and carved a life out of the land. This period also marked the late stages of the colorful steamboat days. These boats powered by steam traveled down the Mississippi and Missouri Rivers, bringing goods, visitors, and new settlers.

These were also some of the last years for Native Americans living in Iowa. By 1851, all lands that had once belonged to Iowa's Native Americans became the property of the US government. In 1857, a band of Sioux warriors attacked a pioneer settlement at Spirit Lake, killing about forty people. The Native Americans were angry over the loss of

Steamboats carried people and cargo along the Mississippi River in the nineteenth century, and sometimes they took part in races.

This advertisement promoted the Underground Railroad and not a ride on any train.

LIBERTY LINE.

NEW ARRANGEMENT---NIGHT AND DAY.

The improved and splendid Locomotives, Clarkson and Lundy, with their trains fitted up in the best style of accommodation for passengers, will run their regular trips during the present season, between the borders of the Patriarchal Dominion and Libertyville, Upper Canada. Gentlemen and Ladies, who may wish to improve their health or circumstances, by a northern tour, are respectfully invited to give us their patronage.

SEATS FREE, *irrespective of color.*

Necessary Clothing furnished gratuitously to such as have "*fallen among thieves.*"

"Hide the outcasts—let the oppressed go free."—*Bible.*

☞For seats apply at any of the trap doors, or to the conductor of the train.

J. CROSS, *Proprietor.*

N. B. For the special benefit of Pro-Slavery Police Officers, an extra heavy wagon for Texas, will be furnished, whenever it may be necessary, in which they will be forwarded as dead freight, to the "Valley of Rascals," always at the risk of the owners.

☞Extra Overcoats provided for such of them as are afflicted with protracted *chilly-phobia.*

their land and the way their culture was changing because of the settlers. The incident was called the Spirit Lake Massacre, and it was the last armed Native American resistance in Iowa. By 1860, very few Native Americans were left in the state.

In 1861, the fight between the Southern states, called the Confederacy, and the Northern states, called the Union, erupted into the Civil War. The main issue that started the war was slavery. Many people in the North did not believe it was right for any person to be a slave. However, many people in the South needed slaves in order to run their plantations. The Southern states voted to secede, or separate, from the Union.

Iowans were deeply involved in the conflict over slavery. When Iowa was made into a state, it had been admitted as a Free State, which meant that it was a state in which slavery was not allowed. However, Missouri, which bordered Iowa to the south, was a slave state. Slaves in Missouri often tried to escape to Iowa. Many slaves were helped to freedom by Iowans who worked for the Underground Railroad. This was a secret network of people who hid runaway slaves and guided them to the Northern states or to Canada.

Iowans helped in other ways, too. During the Civil War, more than eighty thousand Iowans served in the Union army. This gave Iowa the highest percentage (12 percent)

Pioneers make sure everyone knows who owns this land claim in Guthrie in the late 1880s.

Holding Down A Lot In Guthrie.

of its population serving in the military of any state. Though many Iowa soldiers died or were wounded in battle, no battles were fought on Iowa land. The Civil War ended in 1865, and the Southern states slowly rejoined the Union.

A Century of Growth and Change

After the Civil War, several changes opened Iowa's prairie lands to farming. Harder steel blades were made so farmers could put them on their plows and easily cut through the sod. In addition, swamps were drained to create even more farmland. By draining the swamps, though, farmers were contributing to long **droughts** that were a problem for midwestern agriculture throughout the 1900s. It would not be until the late twentieth century that people found that these wetlands were essential to keeping the environment in balance.

The invention of barbed wire made it possible to build fences around fields without using much wood. This was ideal for the plains and prairies since not much wood was available. Houses were made out of sod instead of wood. The thick sod was cut into large cubes and then stacked like blocks. Wood was needed only for framing doors, windows, and a roof. The whole structure could be built for only about $30.

The railroad also helped prairie settlement. By 1880, more than 5,000 miles (8,047 km) of track crisscrossed the state. This meant that almost every farm was within 25 miles (40 km) of the railroad. Railroad companies brought thousands of immigrants directly

The John Deere Tractor Company built one of the state's first large manufacturing plants in Waterloo.

JOHN DEERE TRACTOR COMPANY
WATERLOO, IOWA

from European and Asian countries to Iowa. These workers cleared the land and laid down the tracks. Some moved west when they were done, but others settled in Iowa. By 1900, all of the state's land was claimed.

In the early 1900s, Iowa became the country's leading producer of corn and hogs. The fertile soil and good climate allowed Iowans to increase agricultural production year after year. Sometimes the farm **surpluses**, or food that the farmers did not need to feed their families and their animals, were so great that the prices for these products fell. In other words, there was more food than anyone needed to buy. In order to sell it, farmers had to keep lowering their prices. This was bad for farmers since they could not make a lot of money to continue to support their farms.

In order to try to stop this from happening again, Iowans tried to grow different kinds of crops, instead of having everyone grow the same things. These efforts to change were only partly successful, though. Soybeans from China were tried by some farmers in 1910, but they did not become a major crop until later in the century.

Industry also became more important after 1900. Many of the manufacturing establishments were related to farming, including railroad cars and tractors. Factories were established in or near the cities, offering jobs to people who did not want to farm. This, in turn, increased city populations. Today, all of the state's cities and large towns have some kind of industry.

Changes in the economy forced many small farmers to abandon their land.

Still, the state's prosperity rose and fell on the profits made mostly from agricultural products like corn and hogs. Around 1917, during World War I, the armies of the United States and its allies (England and France) needed large amounts of food. Along with other states, Iowa's farmers did their best to supply it. During these years, Iowa's farms set production records. This did not last very long, though. In the years that followed the war, Iowa's overproduction led to sagging prices again. There was so much food, farmers had to reduce their prices again.

The Great Depression started in 1929, and it brought with it hard times for millions of Americans. Businesses and banks closed, and millions of people lost their jobs. Without work, many could not afford their homes. Farms in many states, including Iowa, were abandoned because the farmers and their families did not have enough money to continue working the farms. Even if they did, most Americans at the time did not have a lot of money

Hollywood Comes to Iowa

The Hollywood movie *The Bridges of Madison County* was set in Madison County, Iowa. The movie features some of the covered bridges found throughout the state of Iowa. There once were nineteen covered bridges, but only six remain.

Medal of Honor

Iowa senator James Wilson Grimes introduced the bill that authorized the Medal of Honor. The Medal of Honor is the highest military award. It is given by the president, who recognizes the efforts of military men and women.

and could not buy the products. Severe droughts added to the problems of farm families. Crops were lost because of the lack of rain. Many Iowans moved west in search of new opportunities.

The US government established some programs that tried to help Americans during the Great Depression. One of these programs created jobs that improved the country. Many men were sent to different states to build roads and bridges. Others were sent to the forests to work in the lumber industry. World War II also helped the economy. Although many lives were lost during this war, the need for supplies helped to pull the country out of the Great Depression. Iowa farms and factories again provided supplies for the troops.

After the war, many Iowans started moving away from the farmland and into the cities and large towns. They did this to look for jobs with more stable incomes than farming provided. By 1960, for the first time, more than half of the state's people lived in urban areas. They had grown tired of the farm economy that continued to ride the roller coaster of changing prices and profits. Some Iowans gave up on agriculture completely and moved away from the state. During the 1970s and 1980s, Iowa's population decreased by more than 150,000. Entire towns were abandoned.

However, the state experienced a heartening comeback beginning in the 1990s. Many communities began to encourage new businesses to come to Iowa. The skilled workers living in the Hawkeye State were one of the reasons why businesses moved to Iowa. The state is home to several colleges and universities. Not only do these schools produce skilled and educated professionals, but they also attract newcomers to the state. The tourism industry has also improved, and many people come to experience Iowa's frontier history and culture. Farmers have been growing a variety of crops, including soybeans, which make the state an important agricultural producer for the world market.

10 KEY DATES IN STATE HISTORY

1. **8500 BCE**
The first people arrive in what will become Iowa.

2. **300 to 1450 CE**
Ancient people called Mound Builders live in the region. Mound Builders constructed various types and shapes of mounds for religious, ceremonial, and burial purposes.

3. **1673**
Frenchmen Louis Jolliet and Father Jacques Marquette become the first Europeans to reach present-day Iowa. Jolliet was an experienced mapmaker and **geographer** while Marquette was more focused on spreading the word of God.

4. **July 4, 1803**
The US government gains the land that includes Iowa as part of the Louisiana Purchase. The United States paid France more than $11 million and agreed to cancel almost $4 million in debts owed.

5. **May–August 1832**
The Black Hawk War is fought, and Sac and Fox warriors are defeated by the US Army.

6. **December 28, 1846**
Iowa becomes the twenty-ninth state. The process of becoming a state took several years because the US government could not agree on Iowa's boundaries.

7. **October 19, 1857**
Des Moines becomes the state capital. The city had previously been called "Fort Des Moines." Iowa City was the capital prior to this time.

8. **November 6, 1928**
Iowan Herbert Hoover is elected as the thirty-first president of the United States. He serves one term, during which the Great Depression begins. Before his presidency, he had no experience as an elected official.

9. **April 1, 1960**
Census shows more Iowans live in urban areas than in rural areas for the first time, as fewer Iowans are farming to make a living.

10. **May–June 2008**
Cedar Rapids, Iowa City, and other areas experience devastating floods lasting nearly a month and causing billions of dollars in damages.

The chance to make a living farming brought people from many countries to Iowa.

The People

3

Ninety percent of Iowa is farmland. Over ninety percent of Iowa's population is made up of white people who trace their ancestry to Europe. However, that does not mean Iowa is made up of only white farmers. The Hawkeye State has a rich cultural history and a diverse population. Many residents are the descendants of settlers who came to Iowa from countries in Europe, Asia, South America, and Africa. Iowa is also home to many different religious communities.

Native Iowa

Before white settlers came to the region, the only people living on the land that would become Iowa were Native Americans. In the years following the Black Hawk War, though, most Native American groups moved out of Iowa. After the Spirit Lake Massacre in 1857, nearly all of the remaining Native Americans were driven out of the state. In that same year, however, a small band of Meskwaki (Fox) and Sac came back into Iowa and purchased about 80 acres (32 ha) of prairie farmland.

Over the years, the Meskwaki bought more land. Today, the Meskwaki settlement covers nearly 3,500 acres (1,416 ha) of farmland in a fertile river valley in Tama County. This is the only Native American settlement in the state. The Meskwaki are especially

These Meskwaki men were among the many Native Americans who trained at a Marshalltown facility during World War II.

proud of the fact that this is land that they purchased and own. In other states, many Native American settlements are on reservations. Reservation land was set aside for Native Americans by the US government, and in many cases, the Natives were forced to live there after their traditional lands were taken away.

The Meskwaki hold a four-day **powwow** every year in August. This event was originally a religious and social celebration of the corn harvest. By the early 1900s, however, more and more non-Natives came to watch the ceremonies. Today, the traditional dances remain the major part of the Meskwaki Powwow, but the foods, crafts, and costumes are also popular. It is a great opportunity for people to learn about Native American history and culture in Iowa.

The Meskwaki are not the only Native Americans in Iowa. Many Native American Iowans live in cities and towns, working in a variety of industries. Some live on farms in rural areas. Though Native Americans make up less than 1 percent of the population, they are still important to the state.

Diversity

As more of Iowa was opened up for farming, and as the cities and towns developed in the 1800s, thousands of immigrants came directly from different northern European countries, including the Netherlands, Norway, Sweden, and Denmark. Small numbers came from southern Europe as well, such as the Italians and Croatians who came to work in the coalfields of southern Iowa.

These newcomers often settled near people who were from the same part of Europe. This gave them the comfort of sharing a familiar language and customs. In 1847, for example, immigrants from the Netherlands founded the town of Pella. They constructed buildings similar to buildings in their European homeland. This includes a windmill in the town square. Every spring, the people of Pella hold a festival called Tulip Time, featuring costumes, food, crafts, and dances from the nineteenth century.

Dutch settlers made towns such as Pella look like the ones they left back in the Netherlands.

Other ethnic communities celebrate their heritage in similar ways. The large Irish-American community in Emmetsburg has a special Saint Patrick's Day celebration every March. Other annual celebrations include a Danish festival in Elk Horn, called Tivoli Fest; a Nordic festival in Decorah; and a Swedish Santa Lucia Festival in Stanton during the Christmas season.

In the 1850s, a community was built in Buxton, with houses on even plots of land. Freed blacks were offered the chance to live here, and for a time it was a model community for African Americans. The town's population of more than five thousand was nearly 60 percent African American. The rest of the population included Swedish, Italian, and Croatian immigrants. For more than thirty years, beginning around 1880, Buxton's people all got along well. There were few signs of racial tension between people of different ethnic backgrounds. African Americans called it "the black man's utopia." (A utopia is a perfect place where everyone can be happy.) When the economy faltered late in the 1920s and 1930s, though, people of all backgrounds began to leave the state. Today, only about 3 percent of the state's population is African American, and they live primarily in urban areas, including Des Moines and Waterloo.

★ 10 ★ KEY PEOPLE ★ ★

Carrie Chapman Catt

Shawn Johnson

Ashton Kutcher

1. Johnny Carson

Comedian Johnny Carson was born in 1925 in Corning. Carson hosted *The Tonight Show* for thirty years and was one of television's most popular personalities. Carson received six Emmy Awards. His last show in 1992 drew five million viewers.

2. Carrie Chapman Catt

Carrie Chapman Catt was born in Wisconsin in 1859, but she grew up in Charles City, Iowa. Catt's work gathered support in Congress for the ratification in 1920 of the Nineteenth Amendment, which gave all women the right to vote. She then founded the League of Women Voters.

3. Roy Halston Frowick

Roy Frowick was born in Des Moines in 1932. Known as Halston, he was an iconic clothing designer in the 1970s. Halston designed hats before becoming famous for his disco dresses.

4. Shawn Johnson

Born in Des Moines in 1992, Shawn Johnson is an American gymnast who won a gold medal for the balance beam at the 2008 Summer Olympics in Beijing, China, when she was only sixteen years old.

5. Ashton Kutcher

Kutcher was born in Cedar Rapids in 1978. He left college to work as a model and was soon cast in the hit television show *That '70s Show*. He has appeared in many feature films and has produced television shows and movies.

IOWA ★ ★ ★ ★ ★ ★

6. Ann Landers

Ann Landers was born under the name Esther Lederer in Sioux City, Iowa, in 1918. She came to be known across the globe by writing a syndicated advice column for the *Chicago Sun-Times*. She gave generations straightforward advice.

7. Cloris Leachman

Des Moines native Cloris Leachman made her television debut in 1948. She has performed in plays, musicals, television shows, and movies. She was on *Dancing With the Stars* at age eighty-two. She won an Academy Award and nine Emmys.

8. Kurt Warner

Kurt Warner played twelve years as a quarterback in the National Football League, winning a Super Bowl with the St. Louis Rams. He was twenty-seven when he played his first NFL game. Born in Burlington in 1971, he played at the University of Northern Iowa.

9. John Wayne

Marion Morrison, better known as John Wayne, was born in Winterset in 1907. He starred in more than two hundred films, usually as the strong, slow-speaking Western hero. He won an Academy Award for his role in *True Grit*.

10. Fred Whipple

Fred Whipple, a professor of astronomy at Harvard University, developed a theory that comets are composed of ice and dust. This was later proved to be correct. He was born in 1906 in Red Oak.

Cloris Leachman

Kurt Warner

John Wayne

Who Iowans Are

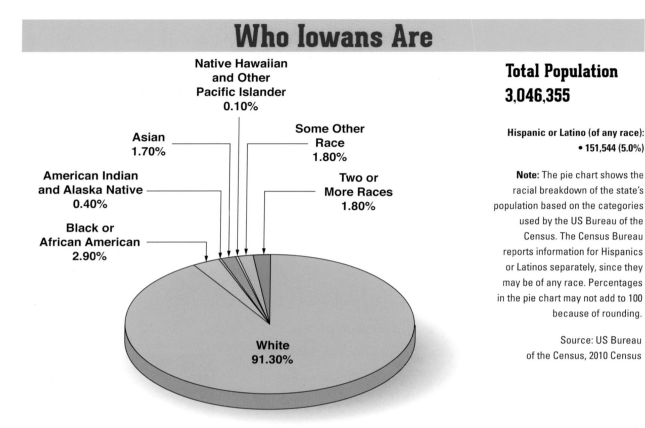

Native Hawaiian and Other Pacific Islander
0.10%

Asian
1.70%

American Indian and Alaska Native
0.40%

Black or African American
2.90%

Some Other Race
1.80%

Two or More Races
1.80%

White
91.30%

Total Population
3,046,355

Hispanic or Latino (of any race):
• **151,544 (5.0%)**

Note: The pie chart shows the racial breakdown of the state's population based on the categories used by the US Bureau of the Census. The Census Bureau reports information for Hispanics or Latinos separately, since they may be of any race. Percentages in the pie chart may not add to 100 because of rounding.

Source: US Bureau of the Census, 2010 Census

Iowa's Hispanic population accounts for about 5 percent of the population. They represent the largest ethnic minority in the state. Some Hispanic Iowans have lived in the state for many generations. Many others are recent immigrants from Mexico and Central American countries. Job opportunities in the cities and on farms are some of the reasons that Hispanics and many others move to Iowa.

Religious Communities

Several religious groups were drawn to the fertile Iowa farmland in the 1800s. Some of the most famous of these religious communities in Iowa are the seven Amana Colonies located southwest of present-day Cedar Rapids. This religious group began in Germany in the 1700s, but their beliefs were unpopular with established churches. They moved to New York in 1842 and then came to Iowa. The Amana Colonies are located on scenic hilly land where they used to live a **communal** lifestyle in which the people all shared the land and all their resources. Although the colonies and people are still there, the traditions and ways of life for the residents have changed and become more modern. The seven closely-knit communities are a major tourist attraction, drawing thousands of tourists every year. The communities are famous for their German-style restaurants and handcrafted woodwork. The Amana Oktoberfest is one of the state's most popular festivals, offering a rich sampling of German foods and drinks, as well as costumes, dances, and crafts.

Another religious group, the Amish, established settlements in southeastern Iowa. As in other Amish communities throughout the United States, the Amish people in Iowa follow simple eighteenth-century ways of living, avoiding most modern machinery. They even drive horse-drawn carriages instead of cars.

Educated Iowa

In Iowa, 90 percent of high school students receive their diploma. The national average for all the states is approximately 81 percent. Iowa also ranks in the top five for average SAT and ACT scores.

The Amish in Iowa are found most prominently near the towns of Kalona and Bloomfield and in Buchanan County. There are approximately seven thousand Amish people in Iowa; they belong to fifty-one church districts throughout twenty communities. The Kalona Amish settlement was founded in 1846. Kalona is the oldest, largest, and best known of the Amish settlements.

The Mormons—members of the Church of Jesus Christ of Latter-day Saints—also set up communities in Iowa. In the 1840s, a large group of Mormons from Illinois moved west and eventually settled in the region that later became Utah. Some decided to stay in Iowa and purchased land in the southern part of the state, around Lamoni. They remained there from 1846 to 1852, and then joined the larger Mormon community in Utah. There are still Mormons living throughout Iowa, though there are no distinct Mormon-only communities.

Education in Iowa

Iowans are proud of the state's long tradition of excellence in education. That tradition began in 1830, when the state's first school was opened. Today, nearly all adult Iowans are literate, or able to read and write. Iowa's high schools boast a 90 percent graduation rate, the highest rates in the nation. Also, 31.8 percent of people ages twenty-five to forty-four years old have a bachelor's degree.

The state also has outstanding colleges and universities. The University of Iowa, founded in 1847, has its major campus in Iowa City. The university is well known for its programs in the fine arts. The university's Writers' Workshop is famous around the world. Emerging writers visit Iowa City to share ideas with one another and with the faculty. The alumni of the Writers' Workshop have won seventeen Pulitzer Prizes. The Pulitzer Prize is an award for achievements in newspaper and online journalism, literature, and musical composition.

Composer, conductor, and playwright Meredith Willson was born in Mason City. He is best known for writing the musical *The Music Man*, which he set in Iowa.

The state's most famous artist, Grant Wood, did much of his work at the University of Iowa, too. Wood was born on a farm near Anamosa in 1891. He moved to Cedar Rapids when he was ten years old. Wood was known for painting the rural Midwest. He said one time that he "got all his best ideas for painting while milking a cow." His most famous work is titled *American Gothic*, which shows a male and female farmer, with the man holding a pitchfork.

Iowa State University of Science and Technology, founded in Ames in 1858, was one of the first schools to offer college courses on agricultural science. It is also a leader in veterinary medicine. Both Iowa State University and the University of Iowa are well known for their sports programs, especially football and basketball.

The University of Iowa is considered to have the top wrestling program in the country, a program that has produced many national champions and Olympic medalists. The University of Iowa holds its home wrestling meets in Iowa City in the Carver-Hawkeye Arena, which holds 15,500 people. In 2015, the University of Iowa and Oklahoma State University wrestled in a special and unique meet in Kinnick Stadium, the school's football stadium. The event was named Grapple on the Gridiron. More than 42,000 fans were present to watch Iowa beat Oklahoma State. This was the largest crowd ever for a dual wrestling meet.

The University of Iowa allows for excellence in both academics and athletics.

Living in Iowa

While Iowa does have several cities, none of them are large compared to many other US cities. Only Des Moines has more than two hundred thousand people. In fact, the ten largest Iowa cities combined total fewer than nine hundred thousand people. The low population density and lack of large cities help Iowa have some of the lowest crime rates in the country. Iowa has the thirty-sixth ranked population density in the country, meaning Iowa is less crowded than more than two-thirds of the other states in the United States.

Grant Wood's most famous painting is *American Gothic*.

The lack of large cities also adds to the impression of Iowa as an example of small-town America. Nearly half the people do live in small towns or on farms. In the past, as settlers moved into Iowa, they purchased their land in what were called quarter sections of 160 acres (65 ha). This created a grid pattern of settlements, much like graph paper or a checkerboard. Today, many property lines in Iowa are still broken up this way.

Small-town architecture with traditional-looking buildings, such as Victorian homes, also reinforces the sense of small-town America. Pride in this nineteenth-century heritage is shown in the many festivals celebrating Iowa's pioneer days, including re-creations of sod houses, nineteenth-century farms, and river steamboats.

The Des Moines Art Center building was designed by I. M. Pei, one of the most famous architects in the world. He also designed the glass pyramid at the Louvre in Paris. The Des Moines Art Center is home to both a museum and a school.

Although more than 90 percent of Iowa's land area is used for farming, Iowans enjoy a lively assortment of cultural opportunities, such as performances by musicians, dancers, and other artists. However, because the population is widely spread out, Iowans often rely on touring groups, or artists who travel from one town to another, for plays, dance performances, and concerts. The universities also serve as cultural centers. Besides offering performances, they also provide training in film, television, dance, and theater.

With its small-town charm, good schools, rich cultural history, fertile farmland, and thriving cities and towns, Iowa has a lot to offer its residents and visitors.

NOTHING COMPARES

JG 13-23 2015

Iowa State Fair

Meskwaki Powwow

1. Burlington Steamboat Days American Music Festival

The town of Burlington has held this summer festival since 1963. This six-day event features music performances, a parade, a golf tournament, and a talent show. In 1986, the event broke a record for the world's longest conga line.

2. Iowa State Fair

The first Iowa State Fair was held in 1854. The fair has been held at its present location in Des Moines since 1886. More than a million visitors come each year to tour some of the eighty buildings or watch competitions.

3. Latino Heritage Festival

Though Iowa's Latino population is smaller than in some other states, this celebration of Latino heritage in Des Moines is the largest cultural event in the state. The festival features music, crafts, and traditional dances from Brazil, Mexico, and Puerto Rico.

4. Meskwaki Powwow

This August celebration, held in Tama, provides an opportunity for people to experience Native American culture. The powwow has displays of crafts, traditional clothing, food, and dances. The one hundredth annual powwow was held in 2014.

Midwest Old Threshers Reunion

5. This event draws more than one hundred thousand visitors to Mount Pleasant on Labor Day weekend. This reunion includes demonstrations of nineteenth-century farm machinery, such as a thresher, and harvesting techniques.

6. National Balloon Classic

More than one hundred hot-air balloons lift off during this nine-day event. Visitors to Indianola get to see the balloons and can even take a ride in one. The event also includes music, food, fireworks and a Nite Glow Extravaganza.

7. RAGBRAI

Each summer, thousands of cyclists enter into the *Register*'s Annual Great Bicycle Ride Across Iowa. The non-competitive race is often considered "part race, part parade, and part party." RAGBRAI has been a summertime tradition since 1973.

8. St. Patrick's Day Celebration

For a full three days in March, Emmetsburg celebrates St. Patrick's Day. Festivities include a Miss Shamrock Pageant, a marathon race, Irish dances, and a variety of food and entertainment including an Irish Baked Potato Bar.

9. Tulip Festivals

During the month of May, the state celebrates tulips. A Tulip Festival is held in Orange City and Tulip Time is in Pella. Both celebrations honor the communities' Dutch heritage. The Pella Historical Society recognizes a Tulip Time Queen and Court.

10. University of Okoboji Winter Games

These winter activities include broomball, snowball softball, a polar bear plunge, a chili cook-off, and much more. The events are centered on the frozen waters of West Lake Okoboji and at Smith's Bay, joining the cities of Okoboji and Arnolds Park.

National Balloon Classic

Tulip Festivals

The dome of the state capitol graces the skyline of Des Moines.

How the Government Works

A s in all states, there are different levels of government in Iowa. Different officials are responsible for a variety of duties. However, one thing is true at all levels: Iowa's government is for Iowans. Iowa citizens elect their officials and the officials work toward addressing Iowans' needs and concerns.

Iowa's cities and towns are grouped by location to form counties. Iowa is divided into ninety-nine counties, and almost all of them are governed by a three-member board of supervisors. Linn County has had five supervisors on its board since 2006, but some residents want to return to a three-person board. Elections for these positions take place every four years. The county government collects city, school, county, and state taxes. The supervisors are responsible for local streets and roads, and they supervise the work of the sheriff's department, the county treasurer, the county attorney, and the courts.

Each town and city in Iowa also has its own government. Cities in Iowa are governed in two ways. In some areas, an elected city council makes the laws that the cities will follow. In other places, a mayor or city manager acts as the executive of the city. Responsibilities for cities and towns include supervising city agencies such as police and fire departments.

Higher Levels of Government

Like other states, Iowa has a state government that is divided into three branches: executive, legislative, and judicial. These branches work together to make the laws and to make sure that the laws are being followed. The executive branch is in charge of enforcing the state's laws. The legislative branch passes the laws. And the judicial branch interprets the laws and settles disputes when they arise.

Iowa is also represented in the federal government through the US Congress. Iowa has two senators serving in the Senate and four representatives in the House of Representatives. Every state has two senators in the Senate. The number of members in the House of Representatives is determined by each state's population. This number may change after each US census is taken. The individuals in Congress who come from Iowa work on expressing the needs of Iowans. They do their best to help make sure these needs are considered when changes are made to national laws that will affect the Hawkeye State.

Branches of Government

Executive

The governor is the state's highest official. He or she is elected to a four-year term. There is no limit to the number of terms a governor can serve. The governor appoints the officers of about twenty state departments and agencies. Other top-level executive officers are also elected, including the lieutenant governor, secretary of state, auditor, treasurer, secretary of agriculture, and attorney general. The governor is responsible for seeing that laws are carried out. He or she also approves or rejects laws.

Legislative

The legislature, called the Iowa General Assembly, is made up of two houses. The senate has fifty members and the house of representatives has one hundred members. Committees in both houses hold hearings to consider changes in the law or new laws. Both houses need to approve laws before they are made official.

Judicial

The Iowa Supreme Court, with seven justices, is the highest court in the state. It reviews cases from lower courts, including the court of appeals and eight district courts. The justices of the supreme court help to interpret, or explain, the laws of the state. Lower courts try criminal cases when a crime has been committed, and civil cases, which usually involve people who are suing others for money.

There is seating in the senate chamber for residents who want to witness what their representatives are doing.

From Bill to Law

When a new law is proposed at the state level of government, it is first called a bill. The ideas for bills often come from Iowa residents who have spoken to their representatives. Either a senator or a representative can introduce a bill into the General Assembly. If a senator proposed the bill, then the bill is first discussed in the senate. The bill is sent to a committee, which will examine it. The committee may hold hearings on this particular bill and invite expert opinions from people who are familiar with the subject. Interested citizens and officials of towns and counties who are affected by the proposed law can ask to testify or speak. These people offer their reasons why they either want the bill to pass or why they believe the bill should be rejected. Senators vote on the bill, and if it passes, it is sent to the house of representatives. There, it goes through the same review process.

Once the bill has been approved by both houses, the governor signs it, and the bill becomes a law. If the governor does not agree with the bill, he or she can veto it. The bill can still pass if the General Assembly overrides the governor's veto. This happens if two-thirds of the members of each house vote in favor of the bill.

Silly Law

One is left to wonder how this law came about, but Marshalltown, Iowa, has an odd ordinance. In this town, horses are forbidden from eating fire hydrants.

Election campaigns get heated before the Iowa caucuses.

Iowa Caucus

Iowa has an important role in national politics. The Iowa caucuses are the first major event leading to determining a political party's nominee for the president of the United States. A caucus is a meeting of party members to select a candidate. There are two major parties in the United States: Democratic and Republican.

In most states in the United States, a primary election is held. During these elections, people cast a vote for the person they want to represent their party. A caucus is different. Instead of going to the polls to cast a vote, Iowans gather at set locations in each of the 1,682 designated precincts, or election districts. These meetings typically occur in schools, churches, public libraries, or even people's houses. During the Democratic meetings, people are trying to convince their neighbors to support their favorite candidate for president. They then make their choice and send their selection into the party headquarters. The Republicans just take a vote.

The caucuses are the beginning of a long process. After delegates, or representatives, are elected at the caucus, those individuals go to the county convention. Then all ninety-nine county conventions take place, one for each county in Iowa. At the county conventions, they select delegates for Iowa's Congressional District Convention and

State Convention. At these much bigger conventions, the delegates are chosen for the presidential nominating conventions.

This whole process takes a number of months, but it's important to remember that the Iowa caucus marks the beginning of the formal events leading to a presidential election. For this reason, presidential hopefuls usually **campaign** in Iowa. They do this to help make sure the citizens of Iowa know what they stand for and to encourage Iowans to support their cause. In the past, the Iowa caucuses have helped to indicate which candidates for president might win the nomination for their parties. Other candidates may also drop out because they find they are not supported.

In Their Own Words

"I have never understood the Iowa caucus."
—Larry King, television and radio host

Iowa also holds primaries in June of election years and Iowa voters choose one person from a slate of candidates for their party. This means that if there are three candidates on the Republican ballot, registered Republicans choose one of them. Delegates to the national convention are chosen at the state convention.

In the general election, in which votes are cast for local and national offices, Iowans follow the same process as most other states. Iowa gets six electoral votes for president, with all six votes going to the person who gets the majority of the votes cast by residents. A candidate needs 270 electoral votes to win the presidency.

State Agencies

Iowa has a number of agencies run by the state that provide services to its citizens. The main agencies include: agriculture and natural resources, business and economic development, education, health and human services, public safety, and transportation. Each agency has different responsibilities and may have a variety of elected officials.

The Department of Agriculture and Natural Resources is in charge of the land. This department oversees the land and water quality. It also monitors and works on conserving the wildlife. The Department of Health and Human Services oversees many different areas. Within this department is the Division of Tobacco Use Prevention and Control. This division may be active in schools throughout the state. People who work in this agency help with creating programs to prevent youths from smoking or being sold cigarettes.

Terry Branstad: Governor of Iowa, 1983–1999 and 2011–

Terry Branstad was born in Leland in 1946. He became the longest-serving governor in Iowa history when he was the state's thirty-ninth governor from 1983 to 1999. Branstad was the president of Des Moines University from 2003 to 2009. He was re-elected governor in 2011 and has since become the longest-serving governor in US history.

Herbert Hoover: President of the United States, 1929–1933

In 1874, Herbert Hoover was born in West Branch, Iowa, home of the Herbert Hoover Presidential Library and Museum. Hoover organized relief efforts that saved people from starvation throughout the world. Hoover served as US secretary of commerce in the 1920s, was elected president in 1928, and served until 1933.

Henry Wallace: Vice President of the United States, 1941–1945

Henry Wallace was the son of a former secretary of agriculture, a position he also held from 1933 to 1941 under Franklin D. Roosevelt. The Adair County native was elected vice president for Roosevelt's third term but was passed over in favor of Harry Truman in the 1944 election. Wallace ran for president as the Progressive Party nominee in 1948 but didn't receive any national support.

IOWA
YOU CAN MAKE A DIFFERENCE

Contacting Lawmakers

If you are interested in contacting Iowa's state legislators, go to: **www.legis.iowa.gov**. You can search for legislators and their contact information by name, zip code, or district. You'll be able to find ways to get in touch with the state senator and representative for every area of Iowa. Click on the "Legislators" tab near the top of the page, and you can also see the district maps for the state.

To contact your national representatives in the US Senate or House of Representatives, go to: **www.congress.gov**. Scroll down to "Current Members of Congress" and use the drop-down menu to find Iowa. There are links to each senator and representative.

Iowans Against Texting and Driving

Many Iowan citizens and lawmakers have shown a concern in making the roads safer throughout Iowa. Because of pressure from the people, Iowa enacted a law in 2011 to curb texting and driving. The law states that police officers may ticket drivers for texting if they're also being pulled over for another offense.

Citizens are still making their voices heard about wanting an even stricter policy in place. Currently, if police officers see a driver texting, they can't pull the driver over to give him or her a ticket unless the driver is also committing another violation, such as running a red light. Iowa polled its citizens in February 2015 and found that 85 percent of them favor stricter laws to address texting while driving. Forty-five states ban texting while driving, but Iowa is one of only five in which it's not a primary offense.

Some Iowan elected officials have been pleasantly surprised by the push from the citizens for stricter laws. Transportation Committee chairman Representative Josh Byrnes said he supports Iowans only using hands-free devices while driving. Several Iowa law enforcement agencies support stricter laws.

There are many companies that process the food grown in Iowa.

Making a Living

Although much of Iowa's land surface is devoted to agriculture, most Iowans are not farmers. Instead, Iowans work in a wide variety of occupations. Included are food processors who package the crops grown in the state, and workers who make some of the best-known appliances in the United States.

Agriculture

Farming, of course, is a major part of the state's economy. There are about ninety-two thousand farms in the state, and the average farm covers about 333 acres (135 ha).

Prairie grasses that once grew up to 9 feet (2.7 m) tall have been replaced by corn and other crops. No state produces more corn than Iowa. In fact, about 20 percent of the nation's corn crops grow in Iowa. Most of the corn is used to feed livestock, including green corn stored in silos for winterfeed. Corn is also used for cereal. One of the country's largest cereal plants is located in Cedar Rapids, called Quaker Oats. The Quaker Oats plant makes oatmeal, cold cereal, snack bars, rice snacks, cookies, biscuits, and more. Iowa is also a leader in producing corn oil, corn syrup, and popcorn. The country's largest popcorn processing plant is in Sioux City.

These cows were among the nearly four million cattle in the state in 2015. Iowa is one of the US's top cattle states.

Iowa is also a major dairy state, with picturesque dairy farms dotting the hills of northeastern Iowa. Farms in all parts of the state also produce eggs and chickens, and some specialize in raising turkeys, sheep, and horses.

By far, the most important farm animals are hogs. Iowa has a hog population of more than twenty million. Hogs are one of the major sources of farm income, and no state raises more than Iowa. The Hawkeye State is also a leader in raising beef cattle. Beef herds graze the grasslands of southern and western Iowa. Some Iowa farmers buy cattle from western states and then fatten them in Iowa on corn.

In Iowa, soybeans are another major crop. Soybeans are used for cattle feed, but they are also used to make oil, soy milk, and tofu products. Iowa farmers also grow wheat, oats, hay, alfalfa, flax, and rye. The state's chief fruit crop is the apple. In addition, many farm families grow a variety of table vegetables, including sweet corn, potatoes, green beans, onions, and tomatoes.

In Their Own Words

"Iowa is home to teachers, farmers, lawyers, factory workers, and many others who work hard every day to provide the best for their families and their future."
—Leonard Boswell, US representative for Iowa from 1997 to 2013

Iowa's fertile soil and available water are ideal for farming. Oddly enough, the most serious farm problem arises when all the farms have a great year. This surplus harvest—or having too much of certain crops—pushes prices down, which is bad for the farmers. In some years, farmers cannot sell all that they have grown. Since the 1930s, the federal government has offered some forms of help to farmers. At times, the government has even paid farmers to take some land out of production. In other words, the government pays them not to grow as many crops.

Manufacturing and Mining

Industries are an important source of jobs for Iowans. Food processing is the leading manufacturing activity. A number of cities have major meatpacking plants. Canned

Families often join in the harvest.

ham and breakfast sausage are popular products. Factories that process dairy products are scattered throughout the state. In addition, a number of industries manufacture trailers and other farm machinery.

There are a few companies involved in other kinds of manufacturing, too. Electrical equipment, especially household appliances, is important in several cities. Amana is a manufacturer of high-quality refrigerators. Winnebago Industries, headquartered in Forest City, produces motor homes. The Pella Corporation in the town of Pella makes high quality windows, doors, blinds, shades, and other products.

From 1870 to 1920, coal mining grew rapidly in Iowa. Mining no longer plays a major role in Iowa's economy. In the past, coal mines were important because they were used to help fuel the railroads. Coal mining declined for several reasons. Most of the coal in Iowa has been dug out. The railroad companies also began buying coal from other states such as Illinois and Kentucky. Other mineral resources in Iowa include limestone, gypsum, clays, and gravel.

1. Appliances

The Maytag Washing Machine Company was founded in Newton in 1893. It was known for the manufacture of washing machines and other household appliances. Whirlpool bought Maytag in 2006 and is now located in Amana.

2. Corn

Iowa corn farmers grew almost 2.4 billion bushels of corn on 13.2 million acres (5.3 million ha) of land in 2014. Most of the corn seen growing across Iowa is field corn. In an average year, Iowa produces more corn than most countries.

3. Food Processing

Iowa is situated around the middle of the United States. Its location makes it an ideal place for food processing plants, as products can be easily and quickly moved by truck or rail to many major cities across the country.

4. Freight Railroads

Iowa has freight railroads that operate on 3,825 miles (6,156 km) of track throughout the state. Of the eighteen freight railroad companies, five of them are major national companies. These railways are charged with transporting most of the grain produced in Iowa.

5. Hogs

The arrival of the railroads made it natural for Iowa farmers to raise beef cattle and hogs for profit. Today, there are five times as many hogs as people in Iowa. One-quarter of all the hogs in the United States are raised in Iowa.

Appliances

Corn

IOWA ★ ★ ★ ★ ★ ★

6. Limestone

Limestone is one source of Iowa's mining income. Quarries are located in more than half the state's counties. The limestone is used for road construction and for manufacturing cement. Limestone is hidden beneath the fertile soil.

7. Manufacturing

Manufacturing firms employ more than two hundred thousand Iowans. This represents about 14 percent of the state's total employment. Changes in technology have created the need for more skilled employees, who have at least a high school diploma. Pella makes wood windows and patio doors in four Iowa cities.

8. Soybeans

Soybeans are the state's second-largest crop, and Iowa is the country's largest soy producer. Soybeans are used for animal feed and are a valuable source of protein. They are used to make meat substitutes, such as tofu and other high-protein foods.

9. Topsoil

Few places on Earth have been blessed with such deep, fertile soil. The soil, along with Iowa's water and good transportation, have made the state a major part of America's "breadbasket," a good place to grow grains.

10. Tourism

Over the past several decades, residents have discovered that visitors are fascinated by Iowa's history and culture. Communities have spruced up Victorian-era houses and other old buildings, and have opened dozens of historic sites for tours.

Limestone

Soybeans

Recipe for Iowa City Oatmeal Cookies

What You Need

½ cup (118 milliliters) butter

½ cup (118 mL) packed brown sugar

½ cup (118 mL) white sugar

1 egg

1 teaspoon (5 mL) vanilla extract

½ cup (118 mL) all-purpose flour

½ cup (118 mL) whole wheat flour

1 teaspoon (5 mL) baking soda

2 cups (474 mL) rolled oats

½ cup (118 mL) semisweet chocolate chips

½ cup (118 mL) chopped walnuts

½ cup (118 mL) wheat and barley nugget cereal (e.g., Grape Nuts)

What To Do

- Preheat oven to 350°F (175°C).
- Grease cookie sheets.
- In a medium bowl, cream the butter, brown sugar, and white sugar.
- Next, beat in the egg and vanilla.
- In a separate bowl, sift together the two flours and the baking soda.
- Gradually stir the flour mixture into the creamed mixture.
- Add in the oatmeal, chocolate chips, walnuts, and cereal.
- Stir everything together.
- Scoop batter with a spoon and drop onto greased cookie sheets.
- Bake for ten minutes.
- Cool on wire racks.

A lot of the grain grown in the state is transported to processing centers by river barges.

Services

Since the 1970s, the United States, including Iowa, has seen a steady decline in manufacturing. More manufacturing industries have been moved to other countries where labor costs are lower. In addition, many factory jobs once performed by people have been taken over by machines. As manufacturing has declined, the country's economy has become more involved with the service industry. This includes any job that performs a service, such as those involved with health care, sales, hotels and restaurants, schools, and banks. By the early twenty-first century, services made up the largest portion of Iowa's economy, as they did in other states.

The largest service businesses are wholesale and retail sales. For example, a truck loaded with new cars that are delivered to a car dealership is engaged in wholesale trade. One owner of a business (the one making the cars) sells a product to another business owner (the car dealership). Then, when a car salesperson sells a vehicle to a customer, they are making a retail trade. In this case, a business is selling a product directly to a customer. The largest wholesale businesses in Iowa are those that sell tractors, farm

Red Delicious

The apple variety known as Red Delicious originated in Iowa in 1872. Until 1940, Iowa was sixth in apple production in the United States. A devastating freeze in 1940 destroyed almost all of Iowa's apple trees.

machines, and cars to dealers. Other wholesale business involves the distribution of farm products to food processing plants. The state's leading retail businesses include restaurants and grocery stores.

Other service businesses include banking, real estate, and insurance. Banks in Des Moines, Davenport, and Sioux City provide services to businesses throughout the state. Several of the country's largest insurance companies have their headquarters in Des Moines.

Iowans also work in a variety of community and personal services, such as law offices, health-care facilities, and consulting businesses. Other kinds of service workers are paid by the government, including public school teachers and workers in state, county, and local government agencies.

Transportation and communication make up other service areas. Railroads, for example, have been important to Iowa farms and towns since the 1850s. Today, although there is not much passenger service, eighteen railroad companies continue to carry freight throughout the state. In addition, river barges are still important for shipping bulk items such as grain. Iowa is the only state that has two navigable rivers—rivers that can be easily traveled down—on its borders. On the west side of Iowa is the Missouri River, and on the east side is the Mississippi River.

In the field of communications, Iowa has more than three hundred newspapers, with about forty of them publishing daily. The *Des Moines Register* is considered one of the best newspapers in the nation. There are also magazines and other periodicals published in the state. In addition, Iowa has many radio stations and about forty television stations.

Tourism

Tourism has become increasingly important to the state in the past few decades. Iowa has a colorful history, and more and more visitors are drawn to its historical attractions such as the Living History Farms, west of Des Moines. This is an agricultural museum spread out over 500 acres (202 ha). The living demonstrations include re-creations of an Ioway Native American village from 1700, an 1850 pioneer farm, an 1875 village, and a 1900 horse-powered farm. Interpreters in costumes use authentic tools to show changes in farm life and agricultural technology through the years.

In a similar way, the town of Fort Dodge has drawn thousands of visitors with its Fort Museum and Frontier Town. This complete frontier village is considered one of the best pioneer museums in the country. Iowa also has a popular maritime museum, the Iowa Great Lakes Maritime Museum, in Arnolds Park. It includes the *Queen II*, a reproduction

Nature preserves and wildlife refuges attract tourists to the state's breathtaking landscapes.

of the 1884 *Queen*, a paddle-wheel boat that traveled across the Great Lakes for about ninety years.

Iowans have also taken advantage of two popular films. A 1989 movie, *Field of Dreams*, featured a baseball field in the middle of an Iowa cornfield. The diamond made for the film still draws thousands of visitors from every state and from several countries. Another film, *The Bridges of Madison County*, has added to the number of tourists who come to see Iowa's famous covered bridges.

The National Mississippi River Museum & Aquarium in Dubuque, one of the largest river museums in the country, highlights the history of rafting and steamboating on the great river.

The Future

The people of Iowa have taken imaginative steps to improve the quality of their lives. For example, Iowa experiences bitter cold spells in the winter, which makes it very hard for people to get out and have fun. Business leaders in Des Moines found a solution by helping to build a 4-mile (6.4 km) skywalk system. This enclosed walkway connects buildings in the downtown area. People can now walk to restaurants, shopping centers, offices, and theaters without ever stepping outside. Not only are people in Des Moines more comfortable in the winter, but businesses can continue to make money and support the economy. Iowans continue to work together to find ways to make their state the best it can be.

IOWA
STATE MAP

Gitchie Manitou State Preserve

Marble Beach State Recreation Area

Silver Lake

Cayler Prairie State Preserve

Okamanpeedan Lake

Union Slough National Wildlife Refuge

Hayden Prairie State Preserve

Laura Ingalls Wilder Museum

Wonder Cave

Spirit Lake
Trumbull Lake
Lost Island Lake

Swan Lake

Five Island Lake

Mason City

Charles City

Yellow River State Forest

Sioux Center

Spencer

Algona

Clear Lake State Park

Fort Atkinson State Preserve

Effigy Mounds National Monument

Spook Cave

Cherokee

Beeds Lake State Park

Brush Creek Canyon State Preserve

Pikes Peak State Park

Sioux City

Kalsow Prairie State Preserve

Storm Lake

Fort Dodge

Cedar Falls

Oelwein

Dubuque

Crystal Lake Cave

Waterloo

Iowa Falls

Blue Lake

Black Hawk State Park

Iowa Falls

Field of Dreams Movie Site

Preparation Canyon State Park

Carroll

North Raccoon River

Ames

Marshalltown

Vinton

Cedar Rapids

Maquoketa Caves State Park

Clinton

Perry

Mesquakie Indian Settlement

Amana Colonies

Lake MacBride

Harlan

Prairie Rose State Park

Ankeny

Lake Panorama

Saylorville Lake

Newton

Grinnell

Iowa City

Davenport

Des Moines

Elk Rock State Park

Wildcat Den State Park

Desoto National Wildlife Refuge

Indianola

Covered Bridges of Madison County

Lake Red Rock

Knoxville

Muscatine

Council Bluffs

Lake Icaria

Twelvemile Lake

Creston

Stephens State Forest

Lake Darling

Mount Pleasant

Shenandoah

Lake of Three Fires State Park

Rathbun Lake

Honey Creek State Park

Geode State Park

Burlington

Nine Eagles State Park

Shimek State Forest

miles
0   40

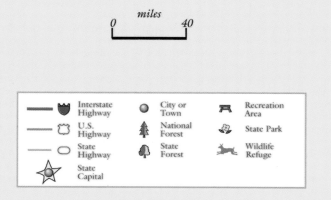

	Interstate Highway	City or Town	Recreation Area
Interstate Highway	U.S. Highway	National Forest	State Park
State Highway	State Forest	Wildlife Refuge
State Capital		

N

W   E

S

IOWA
MAP SKILLS

1. What city is closest to the middle of the state: Clinton, Davenport, or Ames?

2. In what corner of the state is the Laura Ingalls Wilder Museum?

3. True or false: Mason City is in the northern half of the state.

4. Which river runs down the west side of the state?

5. Which city is closer to the capital: Fort Dodge or Sioux City?

6. If you were in Mason City and wanted to go to Iowa Falls, which direction would you have to travel?.

7. Which interstate highway runs through Des Moines, Newton, and Iowa City?.

8. Is Clear Lake State Park closer to Algona or Carroll?

9. Name a city near the southern border of the state.

10. Which cities are closer to each other: Waterloo and Charles City, or Muscatine and Spencer?

Missouri River

Clear Lake State Park

10. Waterloo and Charles City
9. Shenandoah, Creston, Mount Pleasant, or Burlington
8. Algona
7. Interstate 80
6. South
5. Fort Dodge
4. Missouri River
3. True
2. Northeast
1. Ames

State Flag, Seal, and Song

The state flag was designed by Mrs. Dixie Cornell Gebhardt of Knoxville, Iowa, in 1917. It has three vertical stripes—blue, white, and red. In the white center stripe, an eagle carries in its beak blue streamers on which the state motto is inscribed: "Our liberties we prize, and our rights we will maintain."

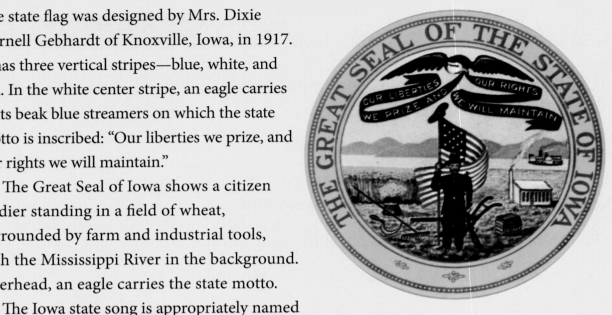

The Great Seal of Iowa shows a citizen soldier standing in a field of wheat, surrounded by farm and industrial tools, with the Mississippi River in the background. Overhead, an eagle carries the state motto.

The Iowa state song is appropriately named "The Song of Iowa." The lyrics were written by S. H. M. Byers in 1897. The Iowa legislature adopted "The Song of Iowa" as the official state song in 1911. The song focuses on the features of Iowa that Byers loved the most.

To see the lyrics to the state song, visit: **www.50states.com/songs/iowa.htm**

Glossary

ancestors	People from whom others are descended; people who came before others in time.
antique	Of or belonging to the past; not recently made.
bluff	A cliff, headland or hill with a broad, steep face.
campaign	To compete for public office.
communal	Used or shared by everyone in a group.
drought	An unusually long period of dry weather, especially one that harms crops.
expedition	An excursion, journey, or voyage made for some specific purpose.
geographer	A person who specializes in the research and study of the natural features, population, or industry of a region or regions.
glacier	An extended mass of ice formed from snow falling and accumulating over the years, moving very slowly.
grotto	A small cave or something made to look like a cave.
loess	Yellowish-gray loam, made up of silt, sand, and clay, that is carried by the wind and deposited loosely on the ground.
petrification	The process that turns an organic substance to stone.
pollution	The introduction of harmful substances or products into the environment.
powwow	A ceremony among Native Americans often including feasting, storytelling, and dancing. Also, a meeting where important topics are discussed.
refuge	A place of shelter, protection, or safety.
reservation	A tract of land set apart for a special purpose, such as for the use of a Native American tribe.
surplus	An amount that is greater than is needed.

More About Iowa

BOOKS

Balcavage, Dynise. *Iowa*. From Sea to Shining Sea. Danbury, CT: Children's Press, 2009.

Griggs, Howard. *The Native American Mound Builders*. Infomax Common Core Readers. New York: Rosen Classroom, 2014.

Schwieder, Dorothy, Thomas Morain, and Lynn Nielsen. *Iowa Past to Present: The People and the Prairie.* Iowa City, IA: University of Iowa Press, 2012.

WEBSITES

Iowa Fun Facts for Kids

factfinder2.census.gov/faces/nav/jsf/pages/index.xhtml

The Iowa Legislature

www.legis.iowa.gov/index.aspx

Official State of Iowa Website

www.iowa.gov/state/main/index.html

ABOUT THE AUTHORS

David C. King has written more than seventy books for children and young adults, including several in the It's My State! series. He and his wife live in the Berkshire Mountains, and they have visited most states.

Jackie F. Stanmyre is a former award-winning journalist at the *Star-Ledger* of Newark, New Jersey, who currently works as a mental health and addiction counselor. She lives in Montclair, New Jersey, with her husband, son, and their two cats.

Index

Page numbers in **boldface** are illustrations. Entries in **boldface** are glossary terms.

Index